A LIFE OF PRINCIPLED OBEDIENCE

Albert N. Martin

THE BANNER OF TRUTH TRUST

THE BANNER OF TRUTH TRUST
3 MurrayfieldRoad, Edinburgh EH12 6EL
P.O. Box 621, Carlisle,Pennsylvania 17013, USA

★

© The Banner of Truth Trust 1992
First Published 1992
Reprinted 2001
ISBN 0 85151 634 3

★

Typeset in $10^{1}/_{2}/12$ Linotron Plantin
at The Spartan Press Ltd,
Lymington, Hants
Printed in Great Britain by
Howie & Seath Ltd, Edinburgh

Introduction

*The Lord is my portion: I have said that I would observe thy
words. I entreated thy favor with my whole heart: be
merciful unto me according to thy word. I thought on my
ways, and turned my feet unto thy testimonies. I made haste,
and delayed not, to observe thy commandments.*

Psalm 119: 57–60

What is the heart of true godliness? What is the essence of
true discipleship to Jesus Christ? The Bible's answer is clear
and simple: *the Christian life is a life of principled, conscientious
obedience to God's will as revealed in the Bible.* The passage
quoted above comprehensively and succinctly states the
major ingredients of such a life.

Before we examine this text to see how it epitomizes the
biblical view of the Christian life, I want to underscore *the
central place that obedience has in the religion revealed in the
Bible.* At the very outset of our study I ask the reader to
affirm with me that the only religious truth and experience
worthy of our consideration is that which is validated by the
testimony of the Bible. The opinions and experiences of men
are of no value as guides to religious truth if they are not in
accord with the witness of the Holy Scriptures. Only the
Bible is authoritative in determining what is true and
normative for the people of God. And again and again the

Bible focuses our attention on the central place which obedience has in true religion.

When God created Adam and Eve and placed them in the Garden of Eden, he plainly revealed to them that all of the joy and blessedness which they had come to know would remain only as long as they adhered to a path of obedience to his Word. God gave them a simple and clear commandment: 'Of every tree of the garden thou mayest freely eat: but of the tree of the knowledge of good and evil, thou shalt not eat of it: for in the day that thou eatest thereof [that is, in the day that you cease to obey me with reference to this tree] thou shalt surely die' (*Genesis 2: 16–17*). All of the blessedness of life in the Garden of Eden, a life of unhindered fellowship with God, a life of true love toward both God and men, all would come to a tragic end the moment Adam and Eve wandered from the path of obedience. Tragically, our first parents disobeyed God! And when Adam stepped out of the path of obedience, as their representative he took all of his descendants with him. Apart from the grace of God, every member of the human race is by nature a 'son of disobedience' (*Ephesians 2: 2*). Ours is a race committed to a course of disobedience to the revealed will of God!

The Bible affirms that when the Lord Jesus Christ came to redeem his people, he redeemed them in a path of obedience to his Father. Whereas the first Adam had ruined himself and all his descendants with him by his act of disobedience, the second Adam (Jesus Christ) secured salvation for his elect people in the course of his principled obedience to the will of God. 'For as through the one man's [i.e. Adam's] disobedience the many were made sinners, even so through the *obedience* of the one [i.e. Jesus Christ] shall the many be made righteous' (*Romans 5: 19*). Note also the language of Philippians 2: 8, which teaches that the Lord Jesus, 'being found in fashion as a man, humbled himself, becoming *obedient* even unto death, yea, the death of the cross.'

The Bible clearly teaches that by an act of deliberate obedience to the will of his Father, the Lord Jesus poured out his blood on the cross in order to secure the salvation of a host which no man can number. Obedience lies at the very heart of the redemption accomplished by the 'doing and dying' of Jesus Christ. The Bible, however, does not stop here. The Scriptures also assert that the salvation which Jesus purchased in the course of his obedience, he now confers only in a way that makes all of its recipients obedient subjects of the living God. And thus in 1 Peter 1: 2, the Bible speaks of the people of God as those who are foreknown of God *'unto obedience* and sprinkling of the blood of Jesus Christ.' The blood of Christ is never sprinkled on any man without Christ's saving work bringing that man into a path of obedience to God. This is why the writer of the Letter to the Hebrews can write as he does: 'Though he [i.e. Jesus] was a Son, yet he learned obedience by the things which he suffered; and having been made perfect, he became unto all them that *obey* him the author of eternal salvation' (*Hebrews 5: 8–9*). When the salvation which Jesus purchased is applied with divine power, it produces in all of its recipients a course of principled obedience to the will of God that is reflective of the course which the Savior walked in securing that salvation.

Furthermore, the Word of God describes the people of God as those who 'keep the commandments of God, and the faith of Jesus' (*Revelation 14: 12*). Christians are not self-righteous people who think that their imperfect obedience is the basis of their salvation – no, they cling to 'the faith of Jesus,' the first rudiments of which is to confess one's own sinfulness and inability to save oneself from the wrath of God upon sinners. And those who acknowledge their sinnerhood and cast themselves upon the mercy of God in Christ – those who keep the faith of Jesus – they also 'keep the commandments of God.' They live lives of resolute obedience to the will of God revealed in his Word. When anyone professes to hold 'the faith of Jesus' and to be a recipient of Christ's salvation and yet obedience is not the basic pattern of his life, God calls such a person a liar: 'Hereby we know that we know him, if we keep [i.e. obey] his commandments. He that saith, I know him, and keepeth not his commandments, is a liar, and the truth is not in him' (*1 John 2: 3–4*).

I hope that the portions of the Word of God cited above are sufficient to convince you that obedience is not a secondary issue – not something that touches, as it were, obliquely upon the heart of true religion. Obedience to the will of God lies at the very center of true biblical religion.

Having, I believe, established that the concept of obedience is central to salvation, we turn now to ask, what do we mean by the term *obedience*? By *obedience* I mean *a conscious, whole-souled conformity to the precepts of God revealed in the Bible, with primary regard to the authority of God which stands behind those precepts*. Perhaps a practical example will help us to understand this definition of obedience. What is an obedient son? When Dad says, 'Son, it's time to come in from play,' do we regard a child to be obedient who, though he actually comes into the house, yet comes pouting and dragging his feet in an evident spirit of rebelliousness? Can you imagine Dad saying, 'Thank you, son. That was a wonderful display of hearty obedience to Dad.' No, of course not. The feet may be coming into the house; but there is no sense that the child believes that Dad has a right to be obeyed because of who he is. At best this kind of grudging, reluctant adherence to parental commands is concerned merely to escape the application of the rod of correction; but there is no true biblical obedience, which has primary concern for the parent's God-given authority. But if the child responds to his father's call with prompt and cheerful compliance, with a cooperative spirit as well as cooperative feet, everyone senses the difference. In such a case there is true heart obedience and not just a kind of reluctant external conformity to parental authority.

Now the obedience which characterized our Lord Jesus in the accomplishment of salvation and which, in the application of salvation, becomes the distinguishing mark of the new hearts of his people is a *conscious* activity. Our Lord Jesus did not float through life, much less go to the cross to die for his people, in a careless and thoughtless manner. His obedience to his Father was conscious and deliberate; and his primary motivation was that his Father, who was worthy to be obeyed, had commanded him to live and die as he did. And this kind of conscious, whole-souled conformity to the precepts of the Word of God, with primary regard to the authority of God, is a distinguishing mark of those who are saved by Jesus Christ. Jesus' true disciples are concerned to live as their Lord lived – as thoughtful and deliberate servants of a worthy Master. And thus obedience, as we shall consider it, is nothing less than conscious, whole-souled conformity to the precepts of God, motivated primarily by the rightful authority of God behind those precepts.

Now it is just this kind of obedience that unregenerate people cannot render to God. Romans 8: 7–8 states: 'The mind of the flesh is enmity against God; for it is not subject to the law of God, neither indeed can it be: and they that are in the flesh cannot please God.' This text teaches us that when unconverted men disobey God's Word, when they are not subject to God's law, their dispute is not with the law of God but with the God who stands behind the precepts of his Word; it is God himself who is the object of the enmity of their carnal minds. Furthermore, this text teaches that unconverted men do not possess the moral ability to obey God or to please God. 'The mind of the flesh . . . is not subject to the law of God, neither indeed *can* it be: and they that are in the flesh *cannot* please God.' The Bible here uses words which denote inability. For the unregenerate man, obedience to God is a moral impossibility. With our understanding of obedience, we can see why this must be so. If true obedience is a matter of the heart and not just a matter of

5

external conformity to the legal code, then surely it is clear that the unconverted man cannot obey God. According to the Bible he has 'a heart of stone.' Before he can obey God in a way pleasing to God, he must have a new heart which delights in God and his Word.

The marvel of God's regenerating grace, the wonder of the new birth, is that God changes the disposition of the heart. One of the great promises of the Bible is fulfilled every time a man or woman is born again by the Spirit of God (*Ezekiel 36: 26–27*):

> A new heart also will I give you, and a new spirit will I put within you; and I will take away the stony heart out of your flesh, and I will give you a heart of flesh. And I will put my Spirit within you, and cause you to walk in my statutes, and ye shall keep mine ordinances, and do them.

New creatures in Christ, who previously would not and could not obey God, have had their native enmity toward God overcome by the mighty regenerating work of the Holy Spirit and they find themselves consciously and wholeheartedly choosing to walk in the path of obedience to God's revealed will.

We come now to a point that is crucial to our consideration of the affirmation that the Christian life is supposed to be a life of principled obedience to God's will as revealed in the Bible. Please follow closely, for this is the heart of the matter! The new birth does not make obedience anything other than conscious, deliberate conformity to God's precepts. The new birth creates a desire to be conformed to God's Word; it gives power to be conformed to God's Word; it creates a new heart inclined to obey God; but it does not alter the basic psychology of obedience. Even for a new creature with a new heart, obedience must involve *a conscious, intentional choice to do what God says*! A pattern of deliberately choosing to obey the Word of the Lord is the very heart of a life of principled obedience. Where obedience is rendered in this fashion habitually (i.e. as a pattern of life), a life of principled, conscientious obedience exists. Where obedience is left to manifest itself according to any other principle than deliberate choice to obey, a pattern of conscientious conformity to the will of God will not exist. The reality of the Christian life is just that simple. The Christian life is not, 'Let go and let God.' It is true that in all our obedience we are to seek and depend upon the power of the Holy Spirit; yet if we 'let go' (i.e. become passive nonparticipants in the war against remaining sin), God will not do for us what He has commanded us to do. God will not obey for us.

We must not permit a life of principled, conscientious obedience to be overturned by unprincipled feelings or by the fact of remaining moral corruption. If our obedience is accompanied by good feelings, wonderful. May God be praised! But if we feel rotten, our duty does not change. If our remaining sin resists us in the path of obedience, we are not excused from our obligation to obey God. And until we embrace this perspective with all of our soul, we will go limping and halting all of our days. Unless we vigorously battle unprincipled emotions and remaining sin, we will know very little of a real life of obedience to God.

Dear reader, what is the case with you? Do you obey God only when there is a comfortable confluence of your feelings and other circumstances so that obedience is something into which you are floated, as it were, on a flowery bed of delights? When your soul is battered by the storm of remaining sin, or your mind is under satanic assault, or your body is weary, do you throw obedience to the wind and live like a pagan? Do you turn from the path of obedience because you don't feel like obeying today? If so, if I have described you, I want by every means possible to turn you away from that mentality. I pray that God will drive that attitude out of your heart and replace it with a spirit of principled obedience that is determined to do the will of God no matter what the cost.

7

What are the roots of a life of principled obedience? If you and I are to render to God a life of conscientious conformity to his will, what foundational perspectives must be present in our hearts? The psalmist tells us the answer when he declares, 'Jehovah is my portion: I have said that I would observe thy words.' Our text displays two of the roots of a life of principled obedience: (1) a saving choice of God – 'Jehovah is my portion'; (2) a determined commitment to serve God and to do his will – 'I have said that I would observe thy words.' Without these two tap roots securely fixed in the heart, there can never be a life of principled obedience.

First, the psalmist affirms that Jehovah, the great God of the Covenant (the God who now has manifested himself to us in the person of Jesus Christ), is his portion. In other words, *he has taken God himself to be the supreme object of his love and devotion.* He has made a saving choice of Jehovah to be his God.

How does the New Testament express this perspective? In order to answer this question as simply and clearly as possible, let us take as our point of departure the so-called 'I-am sayings' of Jesus recorded in John's Gospel. Jesus affirmed, 'I am the bread of life.' The true believer responds from the heart, 'O Lord Jesus, you are my portion of bread: I will feast on you as the only healthful food for my soul.' The Son of God said, 'I am the water of life; if any man thirst let him come to me and drink.' The genuine Christian replies, 'You are the portion of my cup and my inheritance forever.' Christ asserted, 'I am the way, the truth and the life; no man comes to the Father except by me.' The new creature in Christ responds, 'I choose your way, your truth, your life and repudiate every false way; you are my only portion in this world and in the world to come.' This is the very essence of true biblical conversion – to choose Jehovah according to the

8

terms of the revelation which he has made of himself in his Word and in his Son, to embrace him as our portion, as our life.

Dear reader, if you have never seen your sin and recognized your desperate need of God's saving provision revealed in Jesus Christ, if you have never acknowledged your desperate need of that which Christ alone can give to needy sinners in virtue of his perfect life and his sin-bearing death upon the cross, a life of principled obedience to God is impossible for you. All of your determination to live a life of principled obedience will either end in total frustration or you will become a self-deceived formalist, content with outward conformity to a code of decency and a form of religion which may gain the applause of men but which does not please God. In order to do God's will, you first must make a saving choice of Jehovah to be your God.

By God's grace there are many who have made such a saving choice. This, however, is but the first root of a life of principled obedience. Coupled with it is the second – *a determination to serve God and do his will.* If there has been a saving choice of the Lord to be your portion, then there will also be a determined commitment to serve God and to do his will. The psalmist says, 'I have said [as the expression of the deepest resolution of my heart] that I would observe thy words.' The God who is his portion also is his Lord and Sovereign. The psalmist not only has taken Jehovah to be all that he has revealed himself to be as the God of saving mercy; he also has taken Jehovah's words as the rule of his life. Commenting on this passage, Charles Bridges observed:

If we take the Lord as our portion we must take him as our king. 'I have said,' this is my deliberate resolution, 'that I would keep thy words.' Here is the Christian complete – taking the Lord as his portion and his word as his rule . . . All that we are and all that we have, are his; cheerfully surrendered as his right, and willingly employed in his work. Thus do we evidence our interest in his salvation.[1]

Do you have the roots essential to a life of principled obedience? By God's grace have you chosen God himself, revealed in Christ, to be your portion? I am not asking whether you have chosen to live a decent life, or chosen to go to church, or chosen to raise a hand and have an evangelist pray for you. No! Has the Holy Spirit unveiled to you the depth of a need that can be met only in the person and work of the Lord Jesus Christ? Have you chosen him to be your portion? And has there been a determined commitment to serve God and to do his will, a joyful resigning of your will to the lordship of his will, and the choosing of his words to be the rule of your life?

Is this true of you? If it isn't, you have no biblical grounds to say that you are a Christian. And that may be the heart of the problem with you when it comes to trying to live a life of principled obedience. The root of the matter simply is not in you. There has never been a saving choice of God himself and a determined commitment to serve him. And if there has not been, then here and now, while he is yet near in grace and mercy, make the Lord your choice and bow your neck to him. Come under the yoke of the Lord Jesus who said, 'My yoke is easy, and my burden is light' (*Matthew 11: 30*).

2: THE CLIMATE OF A LIFE OF PRINCIPLED OBEDIENCE

Our text not only displays the roots of a life of principled obedience, it also describes the climate in which such a life is lived. And what is the climate, the spiritual atmosphere, of a life of principled obedience? According to our text, there are two elements to such a climate: (1) dependence upon God expressed in real prayer – 'I entreated thy favor with my

[1]Charles Bridges, *Psalm 119: An Exposition* (1827; reprint ed. Edinburgh: Banner of Truth, 1977), p. 143.

whole heart'; (2) faith in God's promised provision – 'Be merciful unto me according to thy word.'

The psalmist first speaks of *a climate of dependence upon God expressed in real prayer*. Faced with the duty of obeying God's Word, he sensed his weakness and proneness to failure and did the only rational thing that he could do under the circumstances – he prayed. With all of his heart he entreated the favor of God. He pleaded that the King would turn his face toward him and give him grace and strength to do his Master's will.

Do you see what the psalmist was conscious of? He knew that it wasn't enough that he had the root of the matter in him. The Lord was his portion and he had sworn himself to obey God's Word. Yet he knew that even the resolution of a renewed heart was not sufficient without present supplies of grace. And so the climate in which his life of principled obedience was expressed was one of prayerful dependence upon God. Only the Lord could give him the power to obey.

The psalmist also speaks of *faith in God's promised provision* as an element of the climate of a life of principled obedience. He prays, 'Be merciful unto me.' But what is the measure of his expectation of mercy? It is the precise size and shape of God's promises: 'Be merciful unto me according unto thy word [i.e. according as you have promised in your Word].'

This is the climate of a life of principled obedience. It is a climate in which there is a recognition that in us (that is, in our flesh) dwells no good thing. The Christian who lives in such a climate acknowledges the truthfulness of Jesus' words, 'Apart from me you can do nothing' (*John 15: 5*). This conviction in turn drives us to entreat the favor of God with our whole heart. Our great encouragement to pray is that God has promised in his Word to provide for us everything we need to do his will. As Peter affirmed, 'His divine power hath granted unto us all things that pertain unto life and godliness' (*2 Peter 1: 3*). God has said, 'My grace is sufficient for you' (*2 Corinthians 12: 9*) and 'sin shall not have dominion over you' (*Romans 6: 14*). According to God's promise, the expectation of the Christian is, 'I can do all things in him [i.e. in Christ] who strengthens me' (*Philippians 4: 13*). Such precious promises become to the believer the very raw materials that he pleads in prayer. He doesn't come and whine before God: 'Oh Lord, I have messed up again; somehow or another, help me to do better.' No. He prays for mercy to be granted according to the very promises of God.

Dear Christian reader, you must learn to cultivate a climate that is conducive to a life of principled obedience, a climate of conscious weakness and total dependence that drives you to pray with your whole heart. Some believers have much work to do in order to cultivate such a climate, especially much work at the throne of grace; but you would never know it by observing the patterns of their prayer life. You can moan and groan about the paltry progress that you are making in grace; but if you will not pray, the tattered garments of a shoddy life will be the token of God's curse upon your prayerlessness. 'You have not,' James says, 'because you ask not.'

God has appointed prayer as the great means of exchanging your weakness for his strength. And if you despise this means, he will not prosper you in your Christian walk. You can run from one elder to another and have a hundred counseling sessions a week; but without prayer, you will make no progress in Christian growth or in victory over remaining sin. Some of you are struggling with besetting sins; yet you don't come daily (even many times a day) asking God to wither the roots of those sins, pleading with him to pour into your heart and mind and spirit the sin-killing virtue of the death of Christ. You don't cry to God with your whole heart; and yet you wonder why you fall so easily before temptation. You make a half-hearted effort to repent and you resolve to do better; and you know that tomorrow you'll be right back where you are today; yet you do not cry out to God with all of your heart. In reality you are playing games with God and with sin.

The climate of a life of principled obedience must be marked by dependence upon God expressed in real prayer and by faith in God's promises. Dear Christian, you must learn how to take God's promises and turn them into fuel for prayer. You must learn how to wrestle in secret with God and how to plead his Word. Without this, you will not know a life of principled obedience.

You may be thinking: 'Pastor, I expected some kind of exotic formula for the Christian life and you have taken me right back to prayer and Bible reading. I heard that when I was just a new baby Christian.' Do you know why you are no further along the road than you are? Because you didn't listen to what you heard. I have taken you back to prayer and Bible reading because that is exactly where our text takes us. The means which God has ordained for growing in grace are simple, not exotic; and if we bypass these simple means – always on the prowl for some magical formula – we are doomed to go limping all of our days.

3: THE ACTUAL PROCESS OF A LIFE OF PRINCIPLED OBEDIENCE

We have looked at the roots and the climate of a life of principled obedience. What now is the actual process involved in living this kind of life? What is the process that goes on in the mind and heart, will and spirit? The answer to this question is set before us in the remaining verses of our text:

I thought on my ways, and turned my feet unto thy testimonies. I made haste, and delayed not, to observe thy commandments.

First, the actual process of principled, conscientious obedience *begins with honest self-examination*. 'I thought on my ways.' These words express the reality of honest self-reflection on the part of the psalmist. He affirms that he consciously and deliberately exercized his mind with reference to his 'ways,' that is, the patterns of his behavior. Our 'ways' are the patterns of our lives – for example, how we spend our time and resources, how we respond to our spouses and children, how we relate to our fellow workmen and neighbors, how we think and speak and act – everything that constitutes the fabric of our lives.

The actual process of a life of principled obedience involves a sober, realistic assessment of where we are. Many years ago a missionary friend was going to a preaching assignment in rural South Carolina and eventually became hopelessly lost. He didn't have any idea where he was, he couldn't find any signs pointing to his destination, and his map was of no help. He was all turned around backwards and didn't have a clue where he was. He concluded, however, that if he could find out where he was, he would be able to find his way to his destination. As he was driving along, he saw a little boy on the side of the road. He pulled over and said, 'Sonny, I'm lost! But if I knew where I was, I think I could get to where I have to go. Can you tell me where I am?' The little boy looked at him with amazement and said, 'Mister, you is right here! That's where you is, right here. You is nowhere else.' God has brought that little boy's words back to me time after time to remind me of the truth that 'right here' is exactly where I am spiritually. What I really am is what I really am and where I really am is where I really am!

Dear reader, do you know where you are? Do you even stop to think? The psalmist apparently wanted to know exactly where he was. He thought on his ways – he reflected on the patterns of his life; and it is evident that he didn't do so in an abstract or superficial fashion, but with the Word of God before him, for he says, 'and I turned my feet unto thy testimonies.' You will never know a pattern of principled obedience unless you are ready habitually to examine where

14

you are with the map of the Word of God open before you. Does that sound like work? You bet it's work. 'Pastor, do you mean that I must do this even when I don't feel like it?' Yes, even when you don't feel like it. 'Do you mean even if I know that I won't be able to avoid the miserable feeling of facing my sin?' Yes, even when the process is painful.

Honest self-reflection in the light of the Word of God, however, is not enough. Self-examination alone will not produce a life of principled obedience. It must be joined to *conscious alteration of one's patterns of thought and behavior.* When you think on your ways in the light of the Word of God and discover sin that needs to be dealt with, does the pain of discovery and the prospect of the spiritual warfare necessary to mortify that sin cause you to turn away from the field of battle? Do you turn on the television or pick up the newspaper or cut the grass, or seek some other diversion so that you won't have to deal with the situation? That's not what the psalmist did. When he discovered a pattern in his life contrary to the Word, a wrinkle that didn't line up right, an abnormality that didn't match God's standard of morality, he set himself to alter his attitudes and conduct. Honest self-reflection led him to *conscious alteration*: 'I turned my feet unto thy testimonies.'

Notice that the psalmist said that *he* did it; *he* turned his feet into the way of conformity to God's Word. He didn't say that he thought on his ways and then prayed, 'Oh Lord, turn my feet.' He said, 'I turned my feet.' In other places in Psalm 119, he prayed that God would turn him. And in our text he has told us that he entreated God's favor with his whole heart. He was a praying man. He lived in the climate of dependance on God's power; but he didn't expect the grace of God to bypass the conscious action of his own will.

What does the example of the psalmist signify for us? It means, for example, that when you've prayed, 'God, help me to keep a pure mind,' and a television program comes on that has scenes that are borderline pornography, you turn the program off! And it means that if you don't have the Christian maturity and will to turn such programs off, you have to get rid of the TV in order to keep a good conscience before God. It means that when you have prayed, 'Oh Lord, help me with my over-eating,' you set clear limits on what goes into your refrigerator and into your mouth, and you start getting on the scales every day and get honest with God. The determination to live a life of principled obedience means that there must be a commitment to conscious alteration of the patterns of one's life; steps must actually be taken to see that the dictates of a biblically informed conscience are implemented at the level of our actual attitudes and behavior.

There isn't a word in our text about feelings—not a word that says altering patterns of sin won't be hard. The psalmist knew that altering ingrained patterns of sin is painful, grueling work. But he also knew that the painful prospect of having to kill sin must not cause the Christian to disregard his duty or to put off his duty to another time. He knew that cowardice and procrastination are the enemies of conscientious obedience to God. This is why he adds, 'I made haste and delayed not to observe thy commandments.' When his conscience was convinced that his behavior was contrary to God's will, he altered his conduct immediately.

When we read the affirmation, 'I made haste and delayed not to observe thy commandments,' we learn that the psalmist was committed to *universal and immediate obedience*. He didn't pick and choose in God's Word as if it were a cafeteria line. He didn't say, 'That looks like an easy thing to do so I'll change that; but that looks too hard, that will mean undoing the patterns of a life-time, that will be like pulling out my own teeth, that will be like plucking out my own eyes.' No! His concern was God's 'commandments' (note the plural) – all of them!

Jesus said that if your eye causes you to stumble into sin, pluck it out, because it is better to enter heaven maimed than having two eyes to go into hell. The bottom line with some of you is that you really don't believe that this kind of radical mortification of sin is necessary. And this is one reason why you aren't making progress. You aren't merciless in altering sinful patterns immediately and universally because somehow you have been deceived into thinking that you can live a loose and shoddy life and still have real confidence that you are a child of God on your way to heaven at last. In spite of all the passages that teach that God's people are an obedient people, you continue in this deception.

Beware delaying to alter any pattern of behavior that comes under the convicting pressure of conscience and the Word of God. The usual result of such delay is hardness of heart. The Bible warns, 'Today, if ye shall hear his [i.e. God's] voice, harden not your hearts' (*Hebrews 3: 15*). What is the connection between the urgency of dealing with sin 'today' and the danger of hardening one's heart? First, ignoring the dictates of our consciences has a deadening effect on our ability to hear the testimony of conscience. City dwellers, long accustomed to ignoring the sounds of city life, no longer hear the noise of traffic. Likewise, men who accustom themselves to ignoring the voice of conscience eventually become deaf to its voice. Second, ignoring the dictates of conscience erodes the force with which our consciences speak. Children who habitually discover that their parents don't listen cease to speak to their parents. Likewise, consciences which are habitually ignored cease to protest with any real vigor against the sins of their owners. Turning a deaf ear to our consciences causes them to exert less and less pressure until the heart becomes hardened to the claims of God's Word.

What a beautiful example we see in David's life of a man who, under the pressure of a tender conscience, made haste and delayed not to deal with sin. King Saul was seeking to kill David. Providence, however, put Saul in a place where David easily could kill him; but David spares Saul's life. Apparently in order later to prove to Saul how easily he could have killed him, David secretly cuts off a little part of Saul's garment. But no sooner has he done this than 'David's heart smote him' that he had acted with disrespect toward God's anointed (*1 Samuel 24: 5-6*). David's immediate response to the smiting of his conscience is to confess his sin to his own men and then to Saul, even though confessing to Saul means making Saul aware of his presence and exposing himself to extreme danger. David made haste and delayed not to have a good conscience toward God and man.

There is nothing in the account of David's confession about David waiting until he felt like doing what was right – not a word about his feelings. David acted on the basis of principle. Dear reader, you are never going to run the Christian race with any strength and consistency until the chains of your feelings are broken. Are you waiting for a wave of lovely emotion to break upon your shore so that you can go riding in behind that wave of beautiful feelings? Are you like the surfer out there waiting, waiting, waiting for the perfect wave? If you are, you will never live a life of principled obedience to God's Word.

A life of principled obedience requires that the perspectives displayed in our text become part of the warp and woof of our character. Some of you grew up thinking that if it didn't feel good, then you didn't have to do it. You were over-indulged by your parents. You weren't made to do anything you didn't like to do. Everything was handed to you on a silver platter. You never had to live with difficulty and hardship like earlier generations. In one sense, you are to be pitied and not blamed that you live by feelings and not by principle. You were short-changed by your parents. In another sense, however, given the light and truth that you now possess, if you continue to live this way, you clearly are culpable and God Almighty will hold you accountable if your feelings-oriented patterns of behavior don't change. Living by biblical perspectives must become a spiritual habit. And if you don't live this way presently, you must start doing so today – right here and right now. If there are matters which need to be made right, don't say 'Lord, tomorrow.' Deal with your sin today. Start living a life of principled obedience now!

4: THE REWARD OF A LIFE OF PRINCIPLED OBEDIENCE

We ought to live a life of principled obedience for its own sake, simply because it is the right thing to do. The will of God ought to be obeyed because it is the will of God. If there were no positive fruits arising from such a life, no rewards attached to it, we ought to be motivated to live in this way simply because it pleases God for us to do so. Jesus, however, as further motivation, spoke of very special blessings – blessings enjoyed in this present life – blessings which come to those who live in conscientious conformity to the Word of God:

> If ye love me, ye will keep my commandments . . . He that hath my commandments, and keepeth them, he it is that loveth me: and he that loveth me shall be loved of my Father, and I will love him, and will manifest myself unto him . . . If a man love me, he will keep my word: and my Father will love him, and we will come unto him, and make our abode with him.[2]

A life of principled obedience constantly affirms and validates the reality of our professed love to Christ. Obedience to Christ manifests the genuineness of our profession. Love, like faith, is displayed in deeds, not in words alone. By our deeds we prove to ourselves that we really are what we claim to be – lovers of Christ and lovers of God. Assurance that we are not hypocrites is a great blessing. And with solid evidence of spiritual reality in the inner man, our hearts can be at rest.

Jesus, of course, takes us a step further. Not only does a life of principled obedience set our hearts at rest that our love

[2] John 14: 15, 21, 23.

for Christ is genuine; *Jesus also affirmed that God is pleased to bless his obedient people by dwelling with them.* The present reward of a life of principled obedience is the privilege of enjoying the presence of God. Present communion with God is a wonderful blessing promised to an obedient people and a great proof that God loves us. His willingness to manifest himself to us and to abide with us is evidence that he loves us deeply.

The Bible promises precious blessings in this life to those who live a life of principled obedience. Do you desire to have solid assurance that you are a real Christian, a real lover of Christ? Do you long to enjoy communion with God and assurance of his love? If your answer to these questions is yes, you will find these blessings only in the course of a life of principled obedience. These are the blessings which Jesus promised to those who obey him.

Did you know that Jesus maintained unbroken communion with his Father by a life of principled obedience? Jesus said,

> If ye keep my commandments, ye shall abide in my love [i.e. abide in the reality and consciousness of my love]; even as I have kept my Father's commandments and abide in his love. These things have I spoken unto you, that my joy may be in you, and that your joy may be made full.[3]

How did Jesus carry about in his holy soul the constant assurance and joy of his Father's love? By living a life of principled obedience. And what did Jesus desire for his disciples? He desired that by their imitating his life of principled obedience, the joy of the blessed communion with God which he possessed would be theirs in rich fullness.

Embedded in the mind and soul of Jesus was a consciousness of the will of his Father. And as he ever reflected upon

[3] John 15: 10–11.

his ways, he turned his feet again and again into the path of obedience. It was his commitment to principled obedience which brought him to the trial of Gethsemane; and it was his commitment to principled obedience which brought him through Gethsemane to the cross of Calvary. When darkness began to press in upon his spirit and he contemplated the cup which he would have to drink, when everything in his holy soul recoiled from the thought of the terrible baptism of abandonment which awaited him, when he cried out 'Father, if thou be willing, remove this cup from me,' when all of his feelings were pulling him away from the path that went to the cross, he said, 'Nevertheless, not my will, but thine, be done.' Jesus' commitment to a life of principled obedience caused him to ride over every natural inclination to shrink back from the agony of cruel crucifixion and from the shame of being hung naked before the rude stare of multitudes. He had to ride over every holy feeling of revulsion at the thought of being severed from conscious communion with his Father – a communion which he had known from eternity and over which there had never come even the least shadow of a cloud. Now he would be plunged into total darkness; yet he said, 'Nevertheless, not my will, but thine, be done.'

Dear reader, if Jesus had not lived a life of principled obedience, we would have no Savior. If Jesus had not been committed to obeying the will of his Father, no matter the cost, he would not have gone to Calvary and died for the sins of his people. But he did obey his Father. He did go to Calvary. And he died to have a people committed to a life of principled obedience. He didn't die to have a people who turn aside from doing his will at every whim and impulse of their feelings, a people who are ruled by their moods. He didn't die to have husbands love their wives only when they feel good, or wives submit to their husbands only when the mood hits them, or children obey their parents only when they want to, or people pray and come to the house of God only when they feel like it. No, Jesus died to have a people conformed to his own moral image of a life of principled obedience.

Do you have the roots for such a life in you? Has there been a saving choice of God and a determined commitment to serve God and do his will? If not, I plead with you, go to God and ask him to give you those roots. Do you live in a climate of conscious dependence upon God expressed in real prayer, and of faith in God's promised provision? Do you engage in honest self-evaluation in the light of the objective standard of the Word of God? Do you make immediate and universal alteration of sinful patterns of behavior, turning your feet into the way of God's statutes?

You may say, 'Pastor, if that is what true religion is, that's too hard, I don't want it.' Well, my friend, your only alternative to biblical religion is to make your own religion. But if you take that course, you must be prepared to perish with your false religion. The only religion which is true and saving is the one which the Bible sanctions. And the only religion which the Bible sanctions is the one which produces a life of principled obedience.

SOME OTHER
BANNER OF TRUTH
TITLES

LIVING THE CHRISTIAN LIFE

A. N. Martin

Have you ever asked, perhaps in a sense of near-despair, 'How can I live the Christian life fruitfully and victoriously?'

Since you so often seem to fail so miserably, should you not listen more carefully to teaching which promises you 'Life with a capital L' ?

Should you not follow the 'secrets' of spiritual living which promise to change you from being a 'struggler' to becoming an 'over-comer' ?

Albert N. Martin faces these questions and answers them squarely from Scripture. He lays down six major principles of genuine spiritual experience, exposes unbalanced and counterfeit teaching, and builds a secure foundation for Christ-centred living.

Written in the vivid, direct and popular style which has made his preaching so widely appreciated and respected, Dr Martin's *Living the Christian Life* contains a vital message for every Christian today.

Albert N. Martin is pastor of Trinity Baptist Church, Montville, New Jersey. This booklet contains the substance of two memorable addresses delivered by him at the Banner of Truth Youth Conference in England in 1984.

ISBN 0 85151 493 X
32pp. Booklet.

THE PRACTICAL IMPLICATIONS OF CALVINISM

A. N. Martin

What is Calvinism and why should it make any difference to the way we live the Christian life? Albert N. Martin's answer is that true Calvinism involves a 'sight of the majesty of God'.

In this compelling booklet, the author describes how Isaiah's encounter with God as the enthroned King brought him to a new awareness of his own sinfulness and the depth of God's forgiveness. As a result, he was overwhelmed by the sovereignty of his holy Saviour and yielded his life to him without reservation.

In the same way, writes the author, Calvinism is 'not . . . whether you have read a book by . . . Kuyper or Warfield' but involves self-examination, self-distrust, practical holiness and prayerful dependence on the Lord.

The Practical Implications of Calvinism is much more than an appeal for Calvinism; in effect it is an impassioned plea for authentic Christianity.

ISBN 0 85151 296 8
32pp. Booklet.

WHAT'S WRONG WITH PREACHING TODAY?

A. N. Martin

The Christian church today stands in need of a recovery of good preaching. But how is that to take place? Part of the remedy lies in seeking to answer the question, What has gone wrong with preaching? The ability to analyse the weaknesses of contemporary preaching (and preachers) is essential to developing healthy and fruitful preaching.

In answering this vital question, Dr A. N. Martin draws on his own experience as a pastor and preacher and on the widespread opportunities he has had to teach and counsel other preachers. Fundamentally, however, his response is rooted in the biblical teaching on the character of those who preach and the message they are to proclaim. *What's Wrong With Preaching Today?* contains a searching message which will disturb complacency; but rather than create despair, it challenges all who preach (as well as those who hear) to rise to new levels of faithfulness and usefulness in the service of Christ.

ISBN 0 85151 632 7
32pp. Booklet.

GROW IN GRACE

Sinclair B. Ferguson

Becoming a Christian is only the beginning of a process of spiritual growth that involves a continual increase in a knowledge of God, an obedience to his word and an understanding of his will. Yet, some Christian's lives seem to grind slowly to a halt, while others are disappointed becuse their spiritual progress has not been as straightforward or as rapid as they had hoped. The growth of others is stunted by a lack of proper spiritual nourishment. Yet others feel they do not understand how to become mature Christians.

Grow in Grace explains how God helps us to develop as members of his family. Taking Jesus himself as the model for our growth, it explains some of the biblical principles of spiritual development, and gives a number of 'case histories' to illustrate how God works in our lives to mature us as Christians.

The biblical teaching in *Grow in Grace* will appeal to Christians at all stages, while its straightforward explanation of the patterns of God's work in his people makes it ideal for those who are just beginning.

ISBN 0 85151 557 6
152pp. Paperback.

TODAY'S GOSPEL –

Authentic or Synthetic?

Walter Chantry

In this arousing work Walter Chantry expounds from Christ's dealing with the Rich Young Ruler the essential elements in Gospel preaching. A close examination of the Scripture evidence leads to this conclusion:

'Differences between much of today's preaching and that of Jesus are not petty; they are enormous. The chief errors are not in emphasis or approach but in the heart of the Gospel message. Were there a deficiency in one of the areas mentioned in these pages, it would be serious. But to ignore all – the attributes of God, the holy law of God, repentance, a call to bow to the enthroned Christ – and to pervert the doctrine of assurance, is the most vital mistake.

'Incredulity may grip you. Can so many evangelicals be so wrong? . . . All are not in error, but great hosts are. All have not perverted the gospel to the same degree, but many are terribly far from the truth. All those who "make decisions" are not deceived, but great numbers are. Above all, few *care* to recover the Gospel message . . .'

This powerfully-written book has a message which goes to the heart of the contemporary problem in a way that conferences and commissions on evangelism have failed to do. Its expository approach is particularly valuable.

Walter Chantry was born in 1938 at Norristown, Pennsylvania; raised in the Presbyterian Church; graduated with a B.A. in History from Dickinson College, Carlisle in 1960, and a B.D. from Westminster Theological Seminary in 1963, and since then has been pastor of Grace Baptist Church, Carlisle.

ISBN 0 85151 027 2
96pp. Paperback.